HAPPY BIRTHDAY, DEAR LUDWIG

Variations in the Style of Beethoven on
"Happy Birthday to You" by Mildred J. Hill and Patty S. Hill

Leonid Hambro

Theme (Bagatelle, Op.119)

Allegretto

Var. 1 (Minuet in G)

Tempo di Minuetto

Var. 2 (Sonata "Pathétique")

Var. 3 ("Moonlight" Sonata)

6

Var. 4 (Für Elise.)

Poco moto

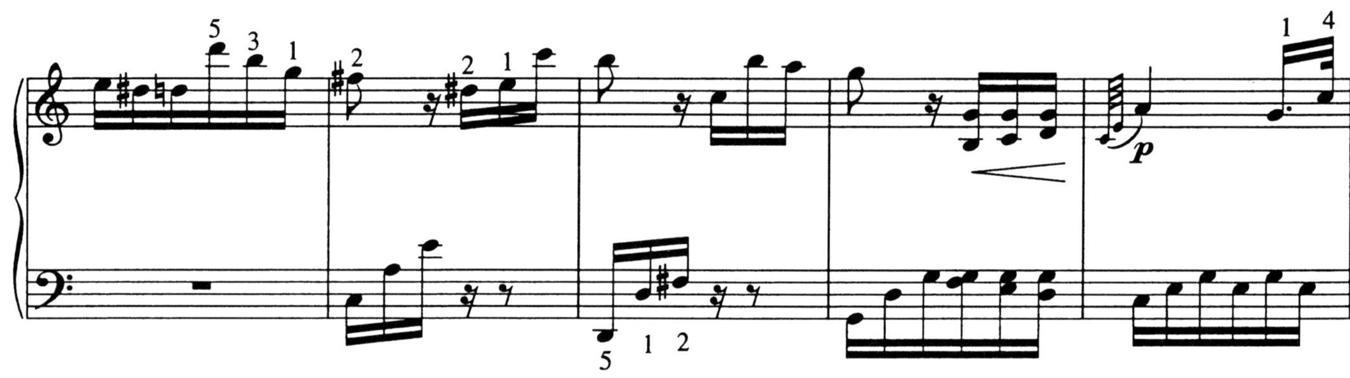

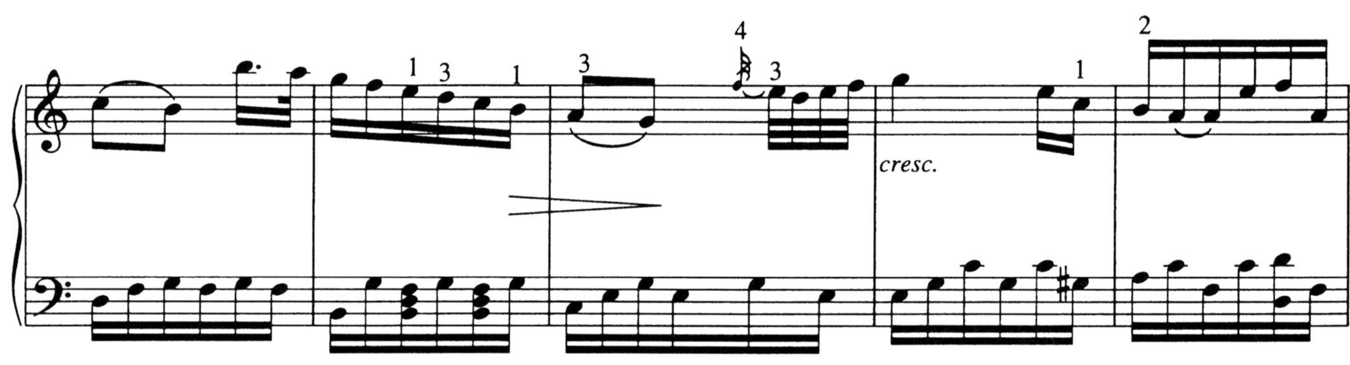

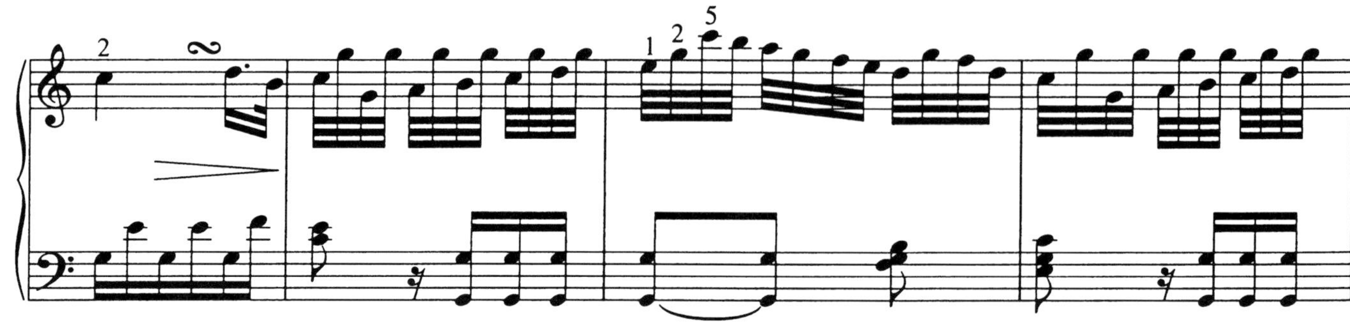

dim e rit.
a tempo
p cresc.
mf
dim

8va
pp

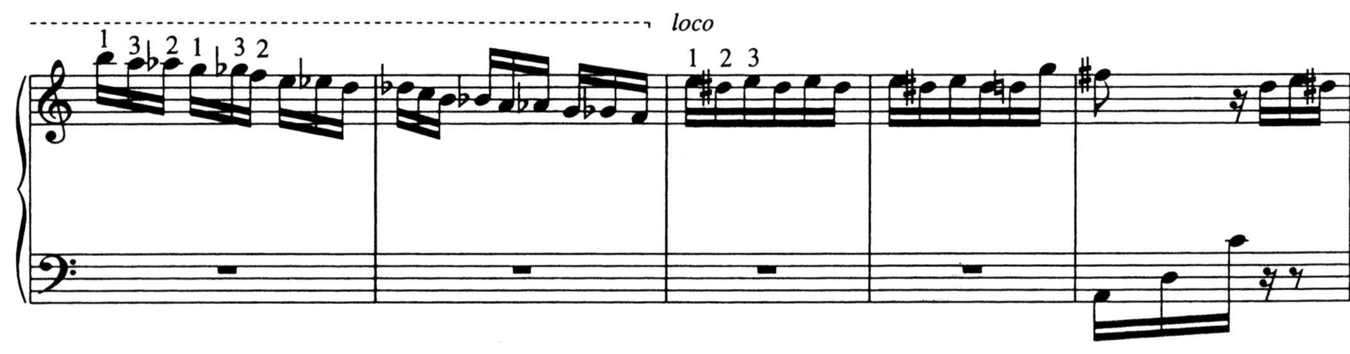
loco

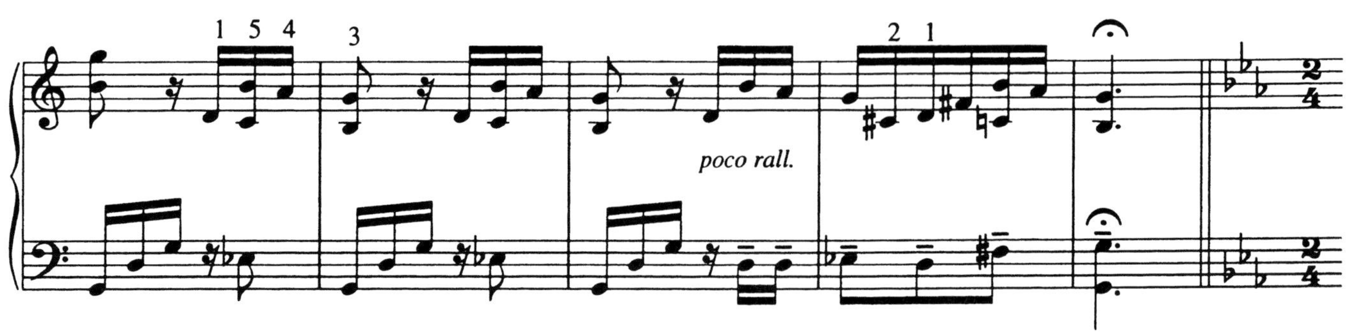
poco rall.

Var. 5 (Symphony No. 5)

Allegro

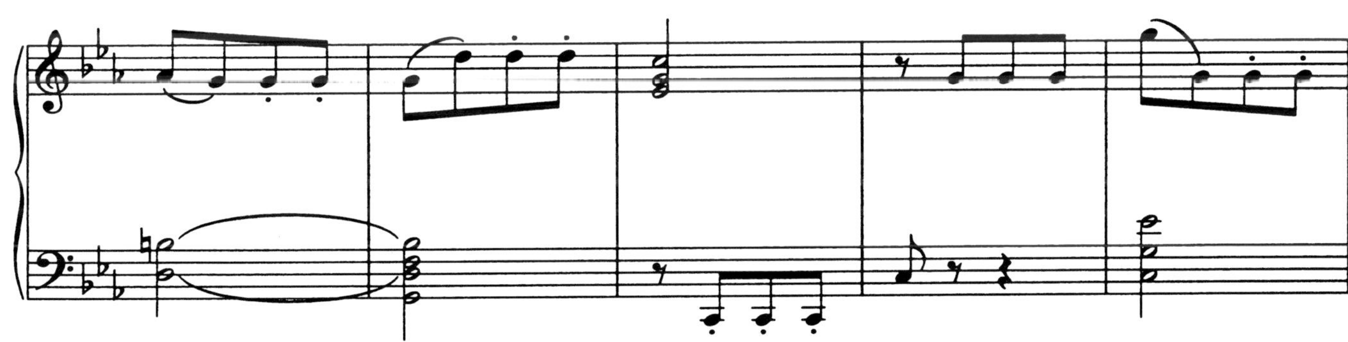

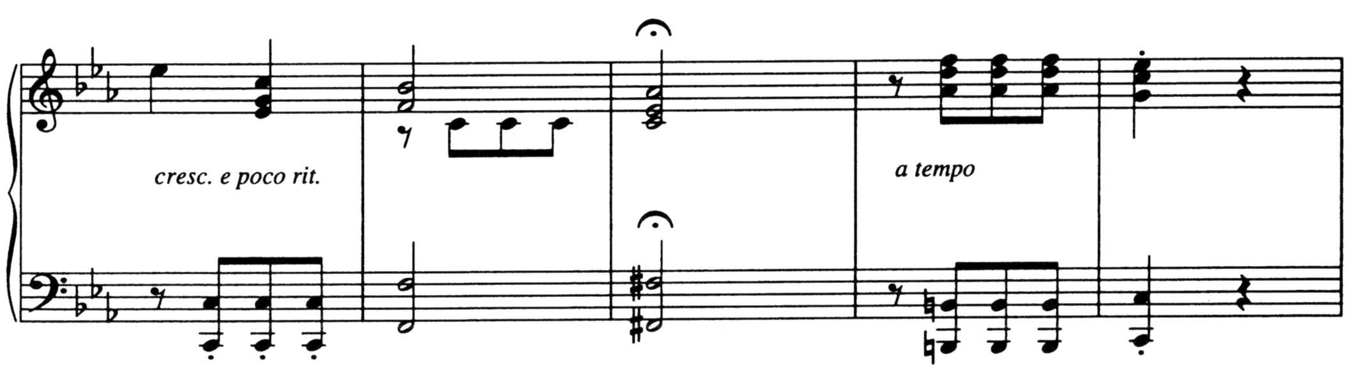

Adagio
ff
rit.
mf
p
a tempo